Say the sounds and blend them together to read the words.

road

bus stop

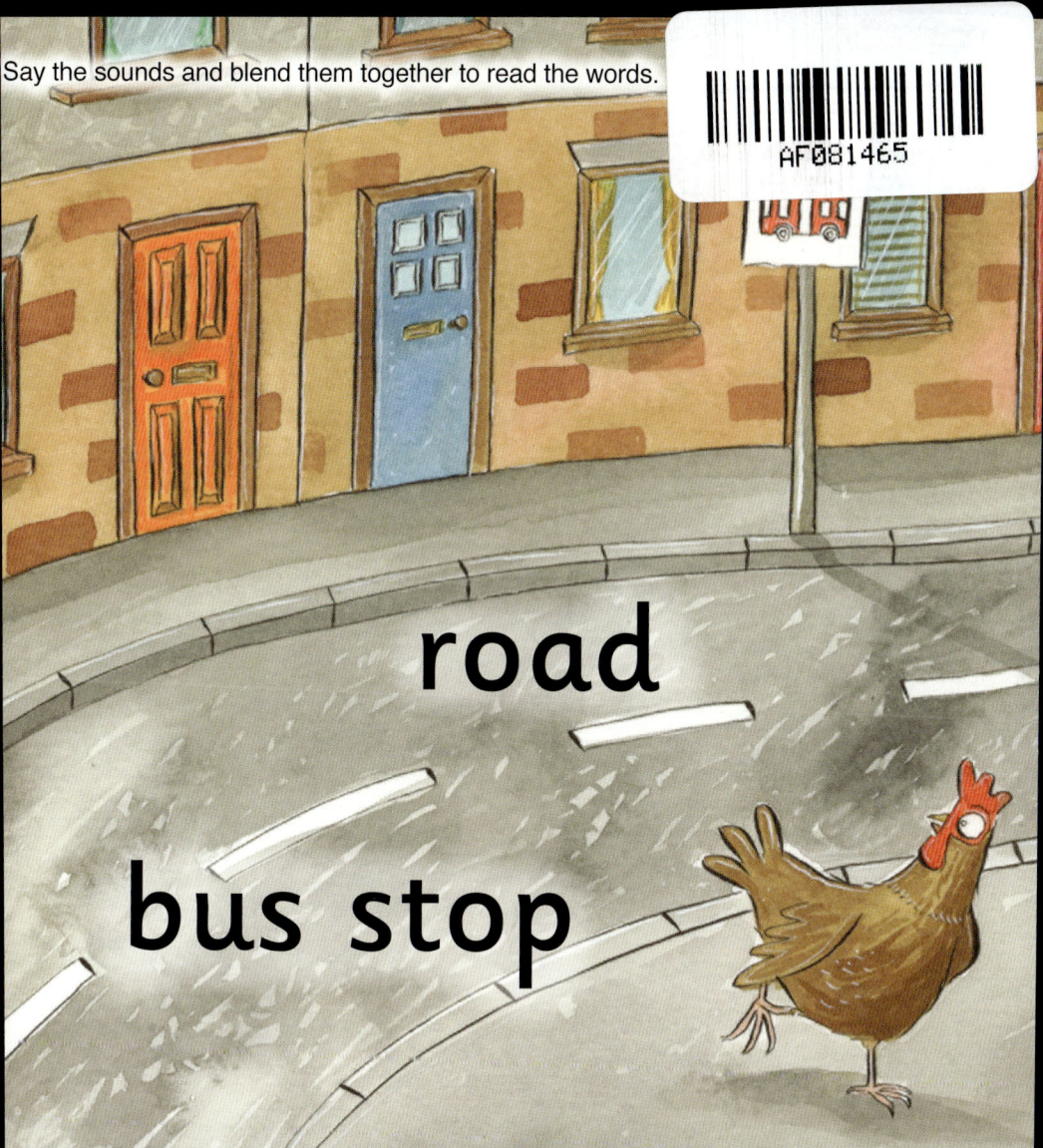

fox

yak

Say the word *van* and listen out for the sounds: *van* – /v-a-n/.
(There is one sound dot underneath the van for each sound in the word.)

chickens crossing

a traffic jam

yelling

Look at the letters and say the sounds.

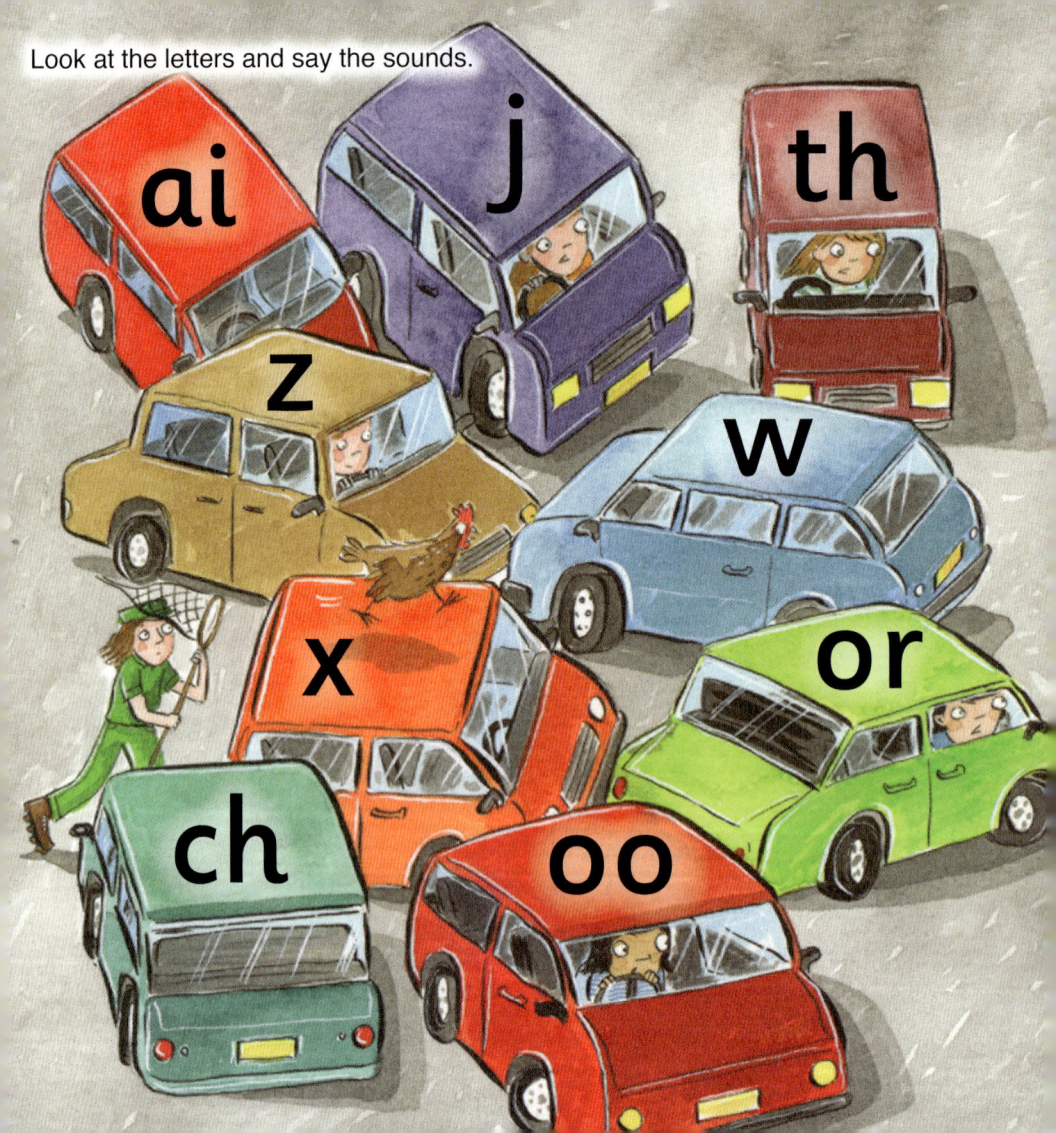

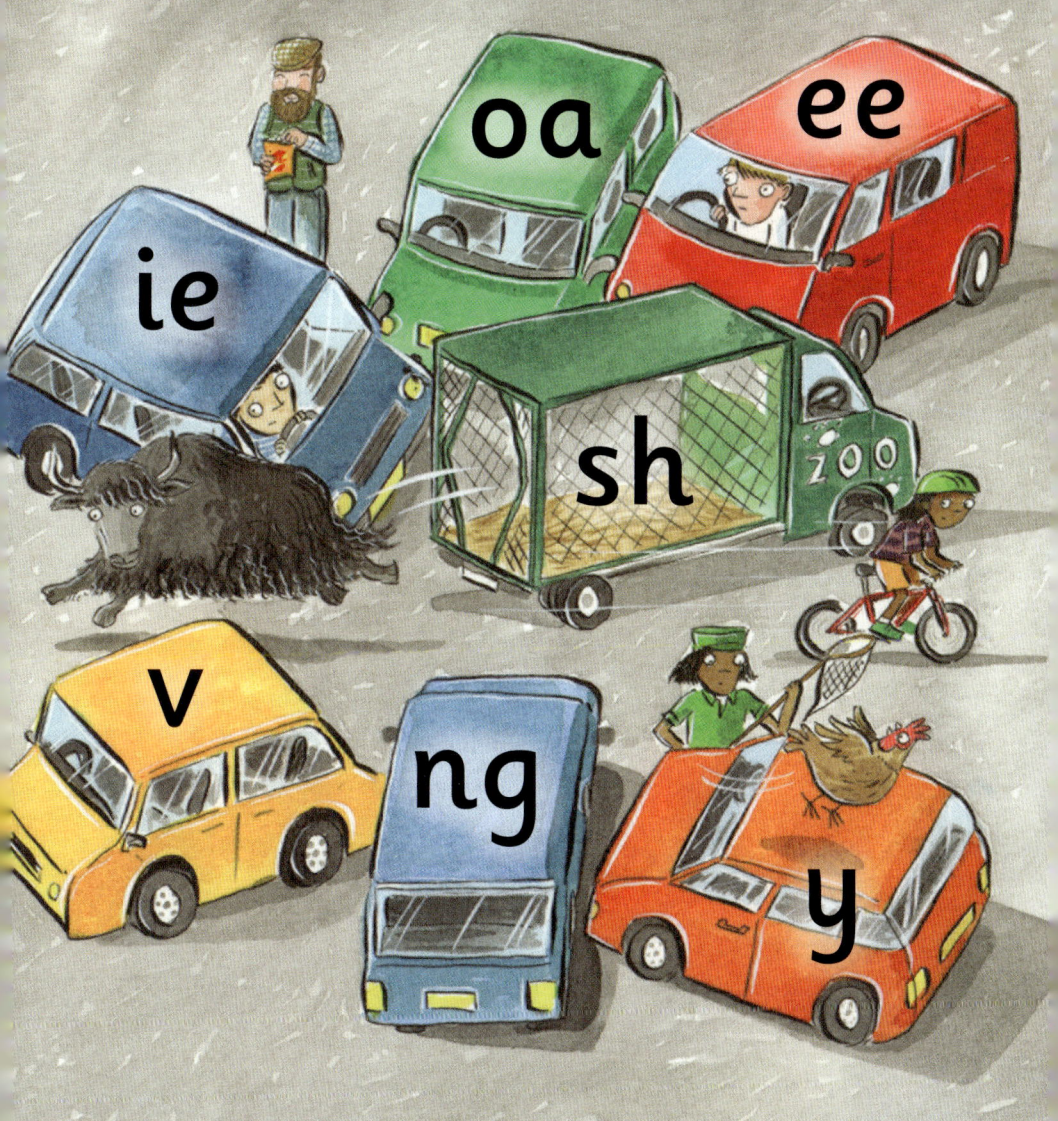

Say the word *bike* and listen out for the sounds: *bike* – /b-ie-k/.